Living Love Quotes

ISBN: 978-0-9980754-4-0

Published by HRI Press, United States 2019
Copyright Todd Huston 2019
No parts of this book can be sold,
copied or transferred in any way
without the express written permission
of the copyright holder.
Photos and art credits shutterstock.
HRI Press

Todd Huston LLC
P.O. Box 702870
Tulsa, OK 74170

www.toddhuston.com

*Dedicated to those who
teach and share their love*

INTRODUCTION

The purpose of this book is to bring an abundance of love into your life. Wherever you are, whatever you are doing, and whatever is happening in your life, these words are to help you reflect on your thoughts regarding love, and to find love.

These quotes came from a lifetime of experiences in speaking, writing, counseling, and interviewing. Each interaction, whether with a group or an individual, has taught me that love is the only way to strength and happiness.

You can read the book in one sitting from front to back, or peruse the book for a couple of quotes that help you move on about your day. I encourage you to find a quiet, peaceful place to read, shut your eyes after a quote or two, and listen to the silence in your mind. You will find inspiration for challenges, solutions for problems, and wisdom for living.

I take great joy in hearing from my readers, and look forward to hearing from you! Share your thoughts and insights with me. Also, if you think of a good quote please send it to me. Who knows, it may find its way into a future book.

May love show in all you do,

*Todd*

if you are wondering
where to find love
look no further
than yourself

*if your* **HEART** *is full of* **LOVE** *so will be your* **WORDS**

# LOVE

THE GREATEST GIFT
YOU CAN GIVE
AND THE GREATEST GIFT
YOU CAN RECEIVE

don't waste time and energy
looking for your greatness
in the world

your greatness is the

*love*

already within you

*love* is the lift in your *wings* that allows you to *soar* to great heights

you were born
to naturally love

anything less than
love
was learned

the only limits to

# LOVE

are imaginary limits

**LOVE** CANNOT BE CONQUERED **NO EVIL** HAS EVER STOOD AGAINST STEADFAST PERFECT **LOVE** AND WON

behind everything you see is a vision of
# LOVE

**HATE** THREATENS TO PUNISH WITH GUILT AND SHAME

**LOVE** PROMISES TO COMFORT WITH FORGIVENESS AND COMPASSION

NOTHING HAS MORE **POWER** TO CHANGE **EVERYTHING** THAN A LITTLE **LOVE**

YOUR GREATEST
CHALLENGES
ARE MERE SHADOWS
FOR
# LOVE
TO CONQUER

# IT'S NOT ABOUT BEING IN LOVE

# IT'S ABOUT BEING LOVE

throw out a pebble of

and watch it ripple
across the sea
the mountains
and beyond

# math is the language of the universe

# love
## is the language of
# life

your rays of

*love*

are greater
than a million suns

**FEAR MOTIVATES FOR A MOMENT**
**LOVE INSPIRES FOR A LIFETIME**

# EXPAND YOUR WORLD WITH THE BROAD BRUSH OF LOVE

EVERY DECISION
HAS ONLY TWO CHOICES

**TO LOVE
OR
NOT TO LOVE**

YOU CHOOSE

IF YOU CHOOSE INCORRECTLY
**LOVE** WILL TEACH YOU
THE LESSON AGAIN

to live a limitless life live with limitless **LOVE**

# love

*not only*

**lights your journey
it is your journey**

with

*love*

as your
compass
you will never
be lost

# TO SEE THE BEAUTY OF LIFE YOU MUST LOOK

# THROUGH THE EYES OF LOVE

TIME AND SPACE
DO NOT CONNECT HEARTS
ONLY

BRINGS
ONENESS

# THE WORLD SEES IN JUDGEMENT AND IS BLIND

# YOU SEE IN LOVE AND ARE ILLUMINATED

# WE ARE ONE FAMILY UNITED IN LOVE

# THIS IS THE ONLY VISION THAT WILL CREATE WORLD PEACE

# YOUR PERFECT BEAUTY IS THE LOVE WITHIN YOU

# LOVE

sings its song for everyone

YOUR SILENCE ALLOWS THE VOICE OF

TO SPEAK

live in love
and you will
sleep in peace

# YOU ARE A POWERFUL BEING OF LOVE

YOU WILL ONLY FIND STRENGTH FROM WITHIN AND THAT STRENGTH IS L♥VE

the
*love*
you give now
radiates
to everyone
everywhere
for all time

send only
love
receive only
love

# Live the one commandment: to

when you
# love
either great or small,
you are doing
the will of God

to fully live
you must
fully love

live your life
full of love

LOVE WHERE THERE IS HATE
AND THERE WILL BE LOVE


LOVE WHERE THERE IS LOVE
AND THERE WILL BE
GREATER LOVE

# LOVE
## IS HEAVEN MANIFESTED ON EARTH

the gift from
# HEAVEN
is

every other good thing is its reflection

*live in greatness by living in*

*love*

your greatest thoughts
will be thoughts of

your greatest words
will be words of

your greatest actions
will be actions of

Be neither deaf
nor blind to life,
look and listen for
the truth of

# WHATEVER BINDS YOU, LOVE WILL SET YOU FREE

# LOVE

*is the lightest load you will ever carry it will lift you to the heavens*

# LOVE
*is not afraid to speak*

live every

moment
in the miracle of
love

the
currency of
# love
has infinite
value and supply

# love

**the more you give
the more you have**

there is no lack of LOVE IN THE WORLD

THERE IS ONLY A LACK OF people sharing LOVE IN THE WORLD

reach out to LOVE SOMEONE TODAY

**love**
takes the
mistakes of the past
to propel you into a life
of infinite possibilities

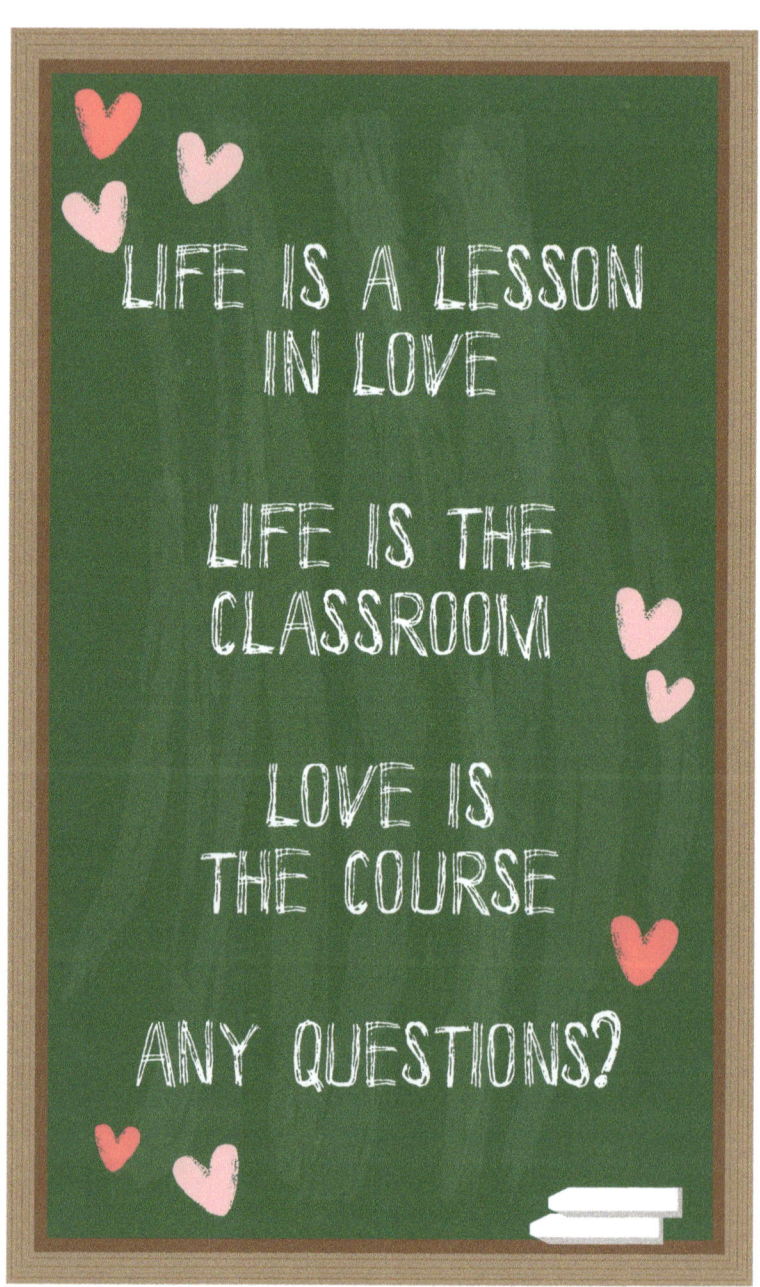

there is a cure for
hopelessness, anxiety,
worry, insecurity,
loneliness,
and fear...
it is not a pill it is

# LOVE

Serving Size 100%

## Side effects include

| Calories 0 | Calories from fat 0 |
|---|---|
| Joy | 100% |
| Peace of mind | 100% |
| Happiness | 100% |
| Mental and physical health | 100% |
| Positive relationships | 100% |
| Laughter | 100% |
| Hope | 100% |
| Cheerfulness | 100% |
| Lightheartedness | 100% |

Other pleasant symptoms related to a wonderful life.

•Percent of Daily Values are based on you. Your daily values may be higher or lower depending on your needs.

*the greatest lesson to teach is the lesson to*

*love*

# THE GRANDEST ADVENTURE

is not into the depths
of the ocean or
the heights
of space but
into the depths of
# LOVE

The most important decision you will make is to **LOVE** all creation unconditionally

THE GREATEST

HAS THE GREATEST

*turn to "the other cheek" of*
**love**

I only fight with

*peace*

it is the only weapon
that heals

*love*

has no
weakness

*love*

is the power
of true strength

*life is better with*
love

LOVE
sees
the innocence
in everyone

**LOVE** IS THE WATER OF LIFE

**LOVE** WASHES AWAY YOUR GUILT, YOUR SHAME, AND YOUR FEARS

**LOVE** PURIFIES THE SOUL

we are over seven billion
beings of **love** ♥
united in **love** ♥
while expressing **love** ♥
in over seven billion ways

what is your expression of
**love?** ♥

**you are a loving
being
living with other
loving beings
in a loving world**

when you deny
your love to one,
you deny love to all

deny no one your love
and you will not deny
love for yourself

# love
## IT DOESN'T NEED TO BE COMPLICATED

we find real beauty
when we see

*love within others*

and within
ourselves

**love** God +
**love** Others +
**love** Yourself =
**love** for All

YOURSELF
TO
FORGIVE YOURSELF

### IF YOU CANNOT

## *love*

### SOMEONE AT THEIR WORST
### THEN YOU CANNOT COMPLETELY

## *love*

### SOMEONE AT THEIR BEST

# SELF LOVE CURES SELF HATE

# LOVE

expresses itself unconditionally to everyone

HATE
IS THE CHOICE
OF THE WEAK

IS THE CHOICE
OF THE STRONG

# Love
## IS
## STRENGTH

there is no power on earth
that can keep your

from shining brightly
in your life and on
the lives of others

the
*love*
you see is the
*love*
you reflect
to find love in all
see love in all

to have **PEACE LOVE JOY**

**GIVE** peace love joy

# love
## IS THE BEST MEDICINE

forgiveness
parts the clouds
and lets the
light of

shine through

the biggest lie is
you are not worthy
of

you are love

and you are loved

your

shines always
just as the sun shines
on a cloudy day

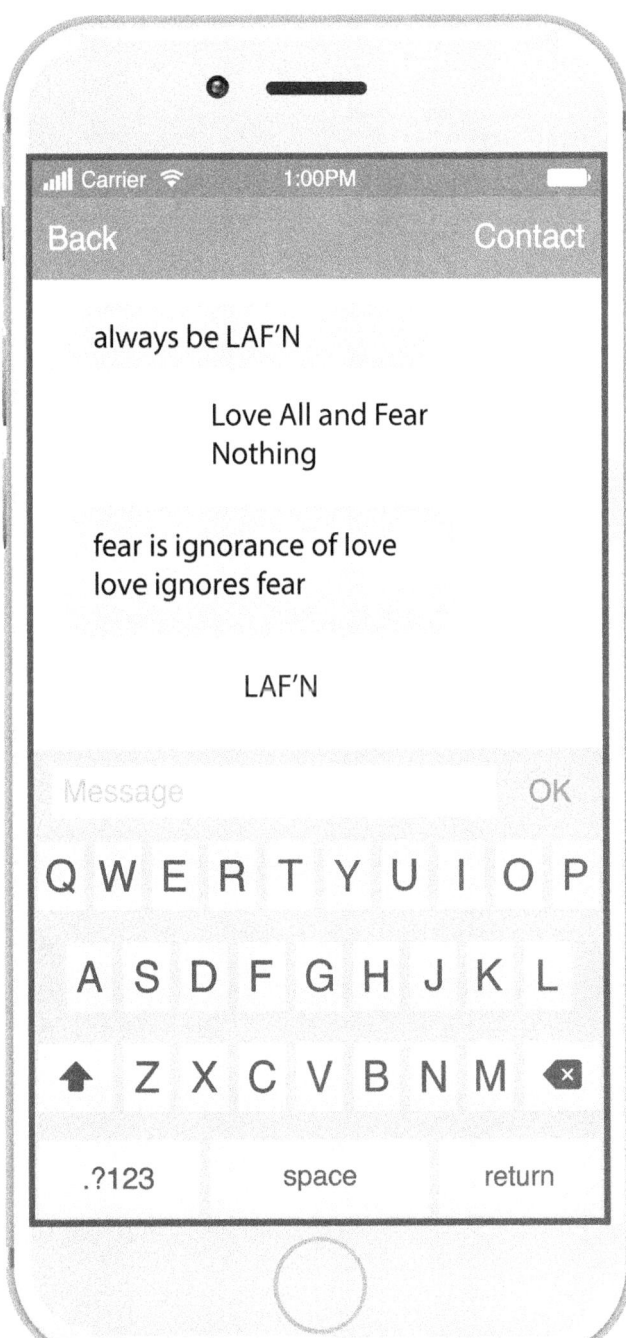

do not let the masks of fear
keep you from seeing
the face of

# love

you are not waiting for

# LOVE
# LOVE

is waiting for you

people may come and go, but

# love

is forever
there is no relationship that

# love

cannot heal

# LOVE
## WARMS THE COLDEST HEART

your gift of
# love
is shared
by you
and others

one pure thought of

# love

can change the world

be the love you are

only one course is required
of you, the course of

*love*

the lessons of love are found
with everyone and in every situation
the object of this course is for you
to have joy and be at peace
and be blessed, if you choose other
than love, love lets you retake the
course, you will ultimately succeed

# LOVE
never quits
and will always
believe in you

# LOVE
wants you to be an expression
of itself in all you think,
say and do

# love
### yourself
## UNCONDITIONALLY

lead and follow with

# love

when you speak with love,
peace will answer you

let love light your path
guide you through your day
and empower your life

compassion
*love*
in action

to

let
# LOVE
be your legacy

tend to the garden of life
sow the seeds of

# love

weed with forgiveness
water with light
then you and others
will rejoice in the
beauty you create

those who fight against you
in hate
will fight for you
in

be not afraid of
love

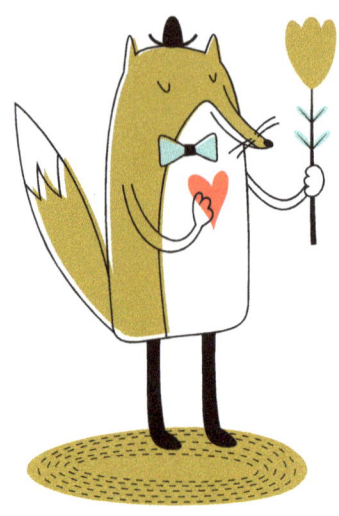

there is only one path in life,
the path of

# LOVE

trust this path and follow it
with all your mind and heart

it will lead you to heaven

to have success in life
find your passion,
follow the path,
be persistent,
and do it with

# LOVE

the person who

and receives

is by far richer
than the richest

all life is equal in

but not all life expresses

equally

the power of

# LOVE

is your only real power
and with it you can create
great change in your life
and in the world

see the world through the lenses of

LOVE

**YOU ARE THE ARTIST OF THIS WORLD, PAINT IT WITH**

# LOVE

# LOVE

does not believe in the impossible
but does believe in the impossible possibilities

# love

is the power
the only power is

# love

nothing is possible

without **love**

everything is possible

with **love**

# love

is your holiness
and perfection
wrapped in
**joy and peace**

There is nothing to fear
but the shadows and clouds
of false thinking

shines light on the shadows
and evaporates the clouds
so you can see clearly

let your life teach

# love

a million illusions
may separate us
but one truth unites us,
the truth of

# LOVE

# love

doesn't distinguish
between those who **love** you
and those who despise you
**love loves** you
**love loves** those who
despise you
**love loves** those who
you despise

## you are always free to choose
# LOVE

may your life be blessed
and full of

# *love*

wherever you go and
in whatever you do *love*
is always with you

Todd Huston speaking at **TEDx**

## LOVE THE POWER

The power of love is our only real power. With it you can create great change in your life, and in the world. Our mission is to (1) educate people of all nations about the best practices of love, derived from scientific research, and spiritual and philosophical traditions, and how it benefits health, relationships, communities, and the world; (2) provide products and services that assist and inspire people to live a daily life of love through their thoughts, words, and actions; (3) be a global movement that transforms all nations, cultures, and societies to live the strength and attributes of unconditional, unlimited love for a kinder, more peaceful, world.

Todd Huston at the palace with the King of Bahrain.
Todd was the keynote speaker for the kingdom's Success Seminar where he spoke to representatives of over 60 nations.

# ABOUT THE AUTHOR

Todd Huston believes the greatest power everyone has is the power of love.

Todd and his wife Julie, their five children, dogs, cats, and fish Phoenix are from Tulsa, Oklahoma. As a leg amputee, Todd became the only disabled person in the world to break an able-bodied world record in sports when he climbed the highest elevations in all fifty states in only 66 days, 22 hours, and 47 minutes, shattering the original record by 35 days. He has traveled the world for over 25 years inspiring people that they, too, can overcome any challenge to reach their goals and dreams.

Todd has spoken from the **Sydney Opera House**, for Middle-East royalty, at **TEDx** events and throughout the United States to Fortune 500 companies. Todd has been featured in thousands of publications throughout the world, including **Sports Illustrated, Forbes,** and the **Wall Street Journal,** as well as the popular book **Chicken Soup for the Soul, A Second Helping.** He appeared as a special guest on **CBS Year in Sports and Robert Schuller's Hour of Power,** and has been interviewed on **ABC, NBC, CBS, CNN, TBN, Inside Edition,** and **Extra,** along with numerous radio programs.

Distinguished honors Todd has received include the U.S. Jaycees Ten **Outstanding Young Americans, Henry Iba Outstanding Citizen Athlete, Class Act Award, The Power to DREAM Achiever Award,** and the American Red Cross **Everyday Hero Award.**

Todd is the author of the book **More than Mountains: The Todd Huston Story.**

www.ingramcontent.com/pod-product-compliance
Lightning Source LLC
Chambersburg PA
CBHW051548010526
44118CB00022B/2629